ESSENTIAL ELEMENTS

FOR STRINGS

A COMPREHENSIVE STRING METHOD

MICHAEL ALLEN · ROBERT GILLESPIE · PAMELA TELLEJOHN HAYES
ARRANGEMENTS BY JOHN HIGGINS

These piano accompaniments can provide helpful guidance for teaching beginning string players. The format includes a cue line to provide the teacher or pianist with a visual guide of the student melody part.

The accompaniments have been arranged to match the style and harmony of the accompaniments heard on My EE Library (www.myeelibrary.com). They may be used for teaching or performance and offer a variety of styles, from classical to contemporary popular music. You may want to alter these piano accompaniments to meet your specific needs. Chord symbols are provided.

ISBN 978-0-634-03821-1

Copyright © 2004 by HAL LEONARD CORPORATION
International Copyright Secured   All Rights Reserved

HAL•LEONARD®
CORPORATION
7777 W. BLUEMOUND RD. P.O. BOX 13819 MILWAUKEE, WI 53213

1. TUNING TRACK

2. LET'S PLAY "OPEN D"

3. LET'S PLAY "OPEN A"

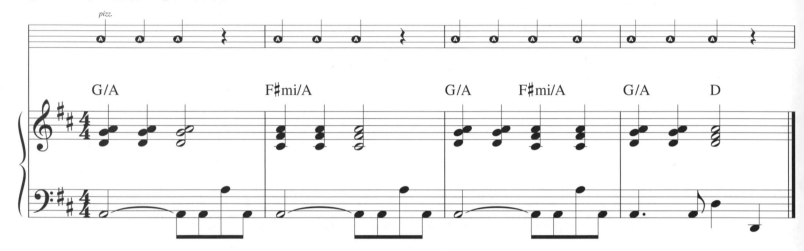

4. TWO'S A TEAM

5. AT PIERROT'S DOOR

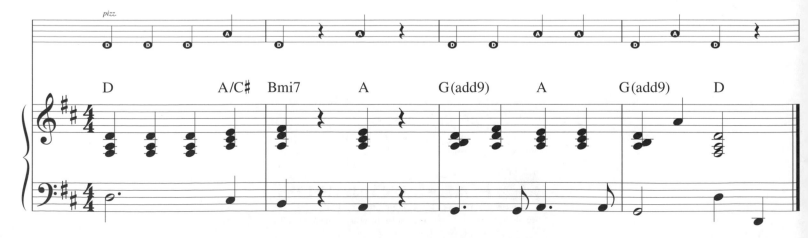

6. JUMPING JACKS

7. MIX 'EM UP

8. COUNT CAREFULLY

9. ESSENTIAL ELEMENTS QUIZ

10. LET'S READ "G"

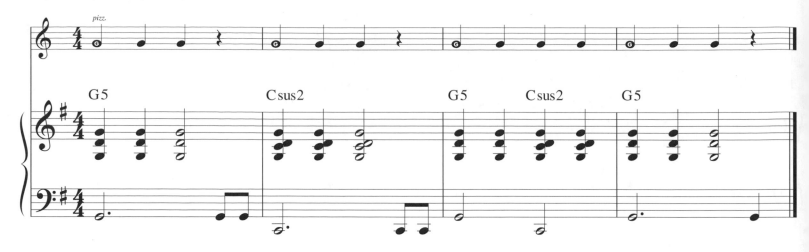

11. LET'S READ "F#" (F-sharp)

12. LIFT OFF

13. ON THE TRAIL

Student books have repeats, not 1st and 2nd endings (until ex. 76).

14. LET'S READ "G"

15. WALKING SONG

Student books have repeats, not 1st and 2nd endings (until ex. 76).

16. ESSENTIAL ELEMENTS QUIZ

17. HOP SCOTCH

18. MORNING DANCE

Slavic Folk Song

*Student books have repeats,
not 1st and 2nd endings (until ex. 76).*

19. ROLLING ALONG

22. ESSENTIAL ELEMENTS QUIZ – LIGHTLY ROW

23. LET'S READ "D"

24. LET'S READ "C#" (C-sharp)

25. TAKE OFF

26. CARIBBEAN ISLAND

Student books have repeats,
not 1st and 2nd endings (until ex. 76).

27. OLYMPIC HIGH JUMP

28. LET'S READ "B"

29. HALF WAY DOWN

30. RIGHT BACK UP

31. DOWN THE D SCALE

32. ESSENTIAL ELEMENTS QUIZ – UP THE D SCALE

33. SONG FOR CHRISTINE

34. NATALIE'S ROSE

35. ESSENTIAL CREATIVITY – *writing assignment in student books*

36. DREIDEL

Israeli Folk Song

41. JINGLE BELLS

J. S. Pierpont

42. OLD MACDONALD HAD A FARM

American Folk Song

43. A MOZART MELODY

Adapted by W. A. Mozart

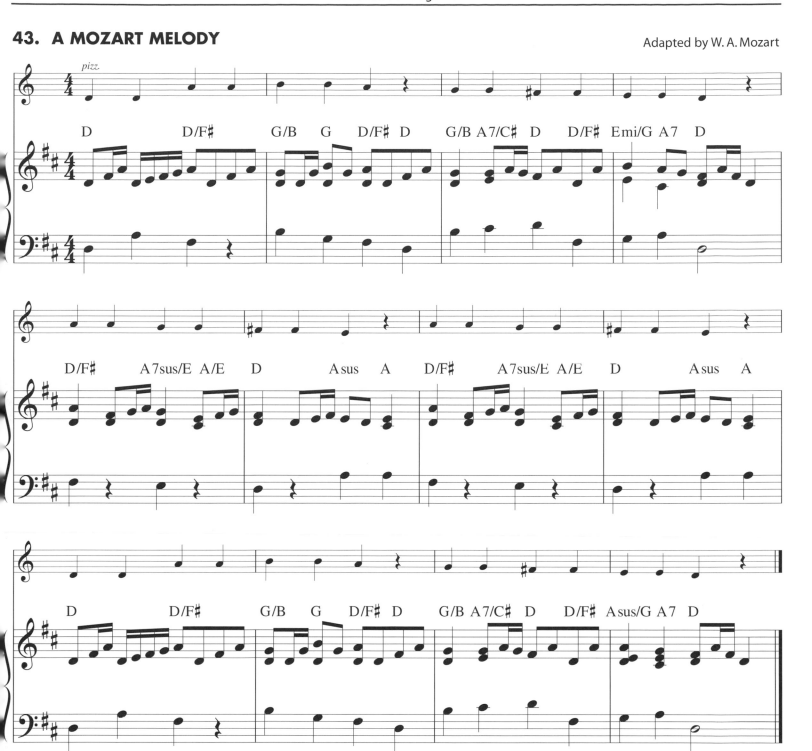

44. MATTHEW'S MARCH

45. CHRISTOPHER'S TUNE

46. ESSENTIAL CREATIVITY – *writing assignment in student books*

47. BOW ON THE D STRING

48. BOW ON THE A STRING

49. RAISE AND LOWER

52. A STRAND OF D 'N' A

53. ESSENTIAL ELEMENTS QUIZ – OLYMPIC CHALLENGE

54. BOWING "G"

55. BACK AND FORTH

56. DOWN AND UP

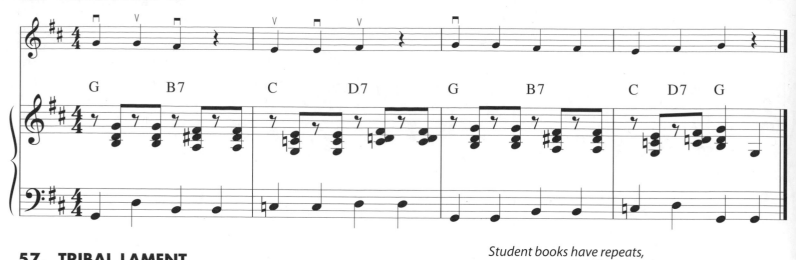

57. TRIBAL LAMENT

*Student books have repeats,
not 1st and 2nd endings (until ex. 76).*

58. BOWING "D"

59. LITTLE STEPS

60. ELEVATOR DOWN

61. ELEVATOR UP

62. DOWN THE D MAJOR SCALE

63. SCALE SIMULATOR

64. ESSENTIAL ELEMENTS QUIZ – THE D MAJOR SCALE

65. LET'S READ "C#" – Review

66. RHYTHM RAP

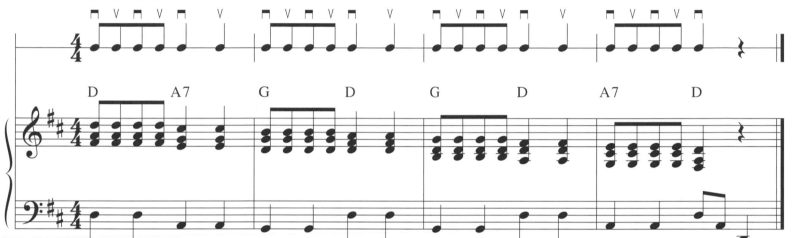

67. PEPPERONI PIZZA

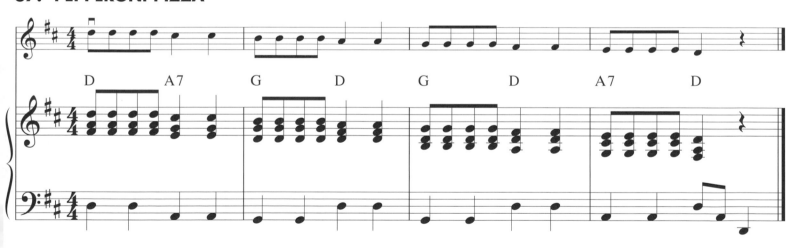

68. RHYTHM RAP

69. D MAJOR SCALE UP

70. HOT CROSS BUNS

Student books have repeats,
not 1st and 2nd endings (until ex. 76).

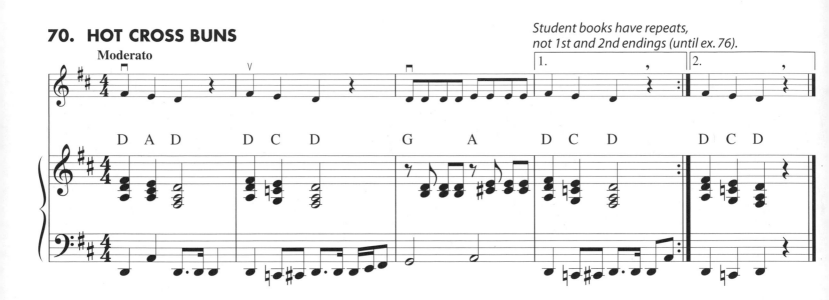

71. AU CLAIRE DE LA LUNE

French Folk Song

72. RHYTHM RAP

Student books have a repeat sign in measure 4.

73. BUCKEYE SALUTE

74. RHYTHM RAP

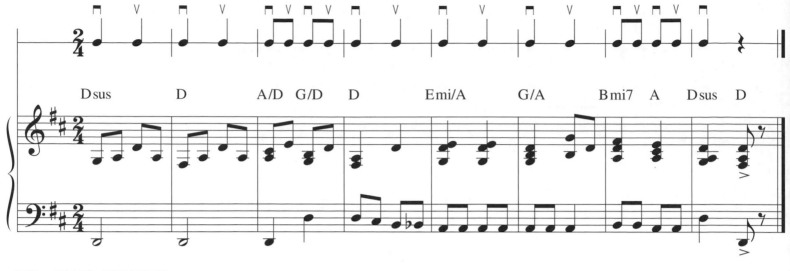

75. TWO BY TWO

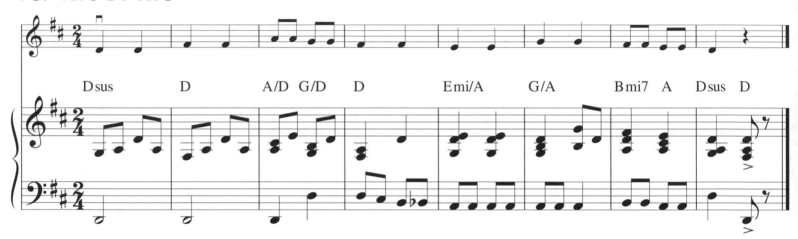

76. ESSENTIAL ELEMENTS QUIZ – FOR PETE'S SAKE

77. RHYTHM RAP

Student books have repeats, not 1st and 2nd endings.

78. AT PIERROT'S DOOR

Student books have repeats, not 1st and 2nd endings.

French Folk Song

79. THE HALF COUNTS

80. GRANDPARENT'S DAY

American Folk Song

81. MICHAEL ROW THE BOAT ASHORE

American Folk Song

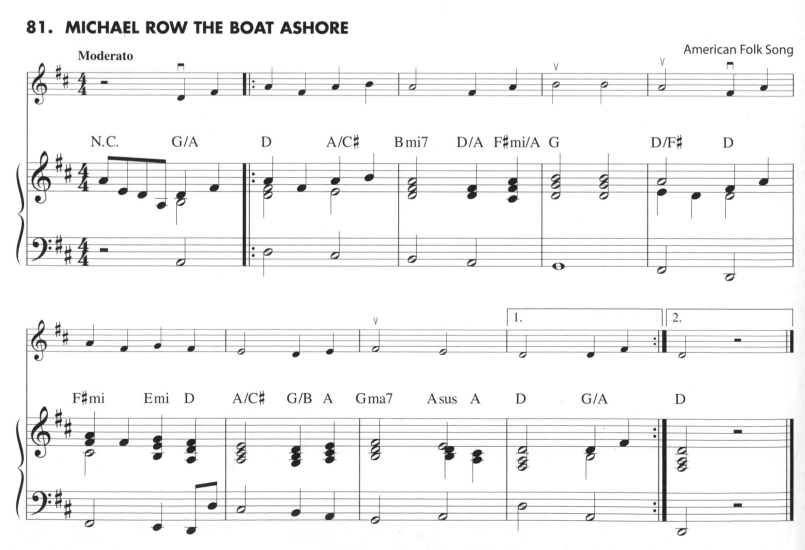

82. TEXAS TWO-STRING

83. FOUR BY FOUR

84. 4TH FINGER MARATHON

85. HIGH FLYING

86. ESSENTIAL ELEMENTS QUIZ – ODE TO JOY

Moderato

Ludwig van Beethoven

87. SCALE WARM-UP

88. FRÈRE JACQUES – Round *(When group A reaches ② , group B begins at ①)*

French Folk Song

Repeat 4 bars on last time (to accompany the round).

89. BILE 'EM CABBAGE DOWN – Orchestra Arrangement

American Fiddle Tune

90. ENGLISH ROUND

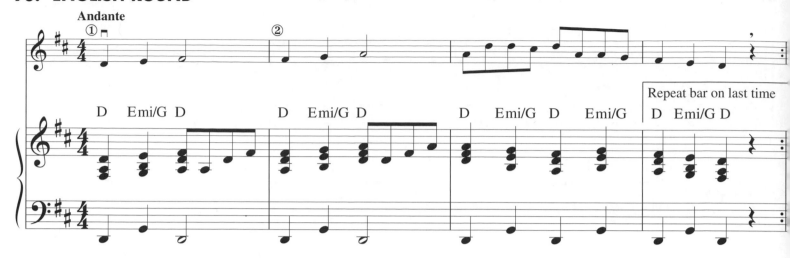

91. LIGHTLY ROW – Orchestra Arrangement

92. CAN CAN – Orchestra Arrangement

Jacques Offenbach
Arr. John Higgins

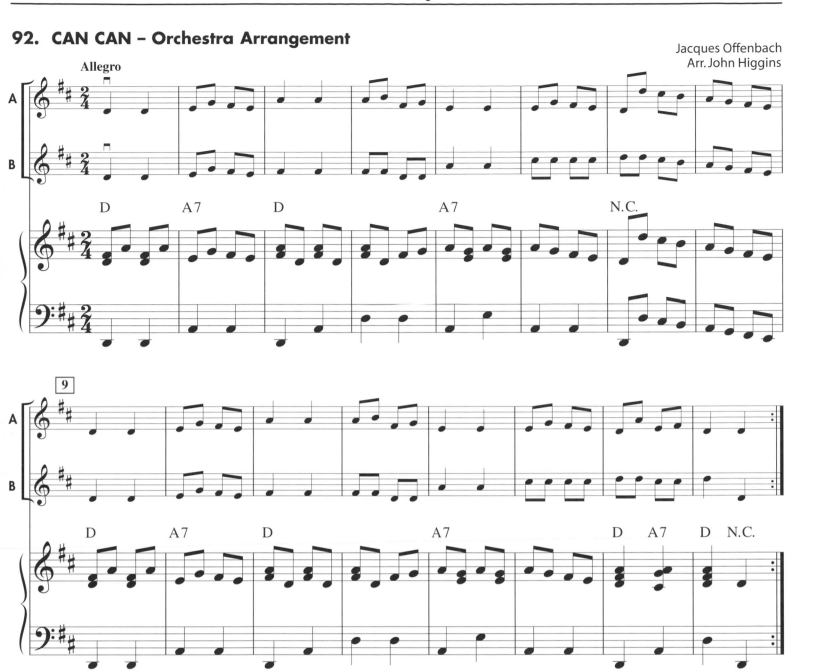

93. LET'S READ "G"

94. LET'S READ "C" (C-natural)

95. LET'S READ "B"

96. LET'S READ "A"

97. WALKING AROUND

98. G MAJOR SCALE

99. FOURTH FINGER D

100. LOW DOWN

101. BAA BAA BLACK SHEEP

102. ESSENTIAL ELEMENTS QUIZ – THIS OLD MAN

American Folk Song

105. D MAJOR SCALE IN THREES

106. FRENCH FOLK SONG

107. ESSENTIAL ELEMENTS QUIZ – SAILOR'S SONG

English Sea Song

108. FIT TO BE TIED

109. STOP AND GO

110. SLURRING ALONG

111. SMOOTH SAILING

112. D MAJOR SLURS

113. CROSSING STRINGS

114. GLIDING BOWS

115. UPSIDE DOWN

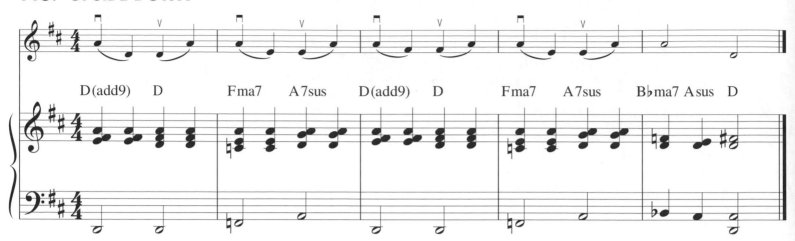

116. SONG FOR MARIA

117. BANANA BOAT SONG

Caribbean Folk Song

118. FIROLIRALERA – Orchestra Arrangement

Mexican Folk Song
Arr. John higgins

119.

120.

121.

122.

123.

124.

125. JINGLI NONA

Far Eastern Folk Song

126. LET'S READ "F" (F-natural)

127. HALF-STEPPIN' AND WHOLE STEPPIN'

Student books have repeats, not 1st and 2nd endings.

128. SPY GUY

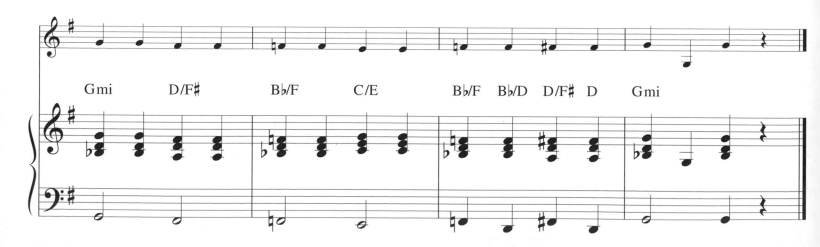

129. MINOR DETAILS

130. LET'S READ "C"

131. HALF STEP AND WHOLE STEP REVIEW

Student books have repeats, not 1st and 2nd endings.

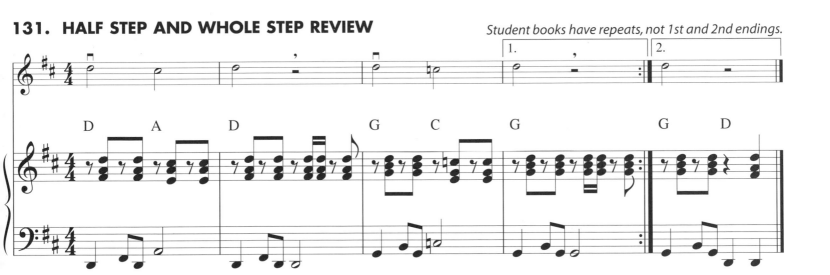

132. CHROMATIC MOVES

133. THE STETSON SPECIAL

134. BLUEBIRD'S SONG

135. C MAJOR SCALE – Round

136. SPLIT DECISION – Duet

137. OAK HOLLOW

Moderato

138. A-TISKET, A-TASKET

Allegro

139. ESSENTIAL ELEMENTS QUIZ – RUSSIAN FOLK TUNE

Russian Folk Song

140. BINGO

18th Century English Game Song

Allegro *Student books repeat to the upbeat before measure 1.*

Student books have repeats, not 1st and 2nd endings.

141. TALLIS CANON

Thomas Tallis

Moderato

Repeat on last time (to accompany the round)

142. VARIATIONS ON A FAMILIAR SONG

Variation 2 – *make up your own variation*

143. ESSENTIAL CREATIVITY – BIRTHDAY SONG

Student *Now play the line again and create your own rhythm.*

144. LET'S READ "C" – Review

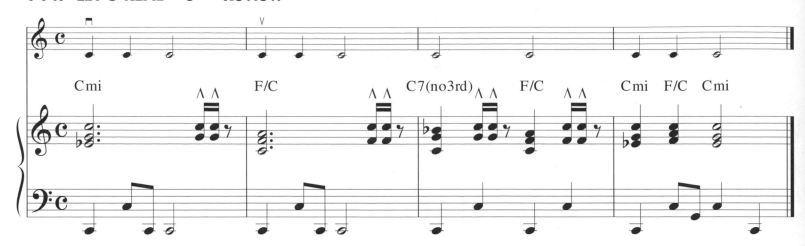

145. LET'S READ "F" – Review

146. LET'S READ "E" – Review

147. LET'S READ "D" – Review

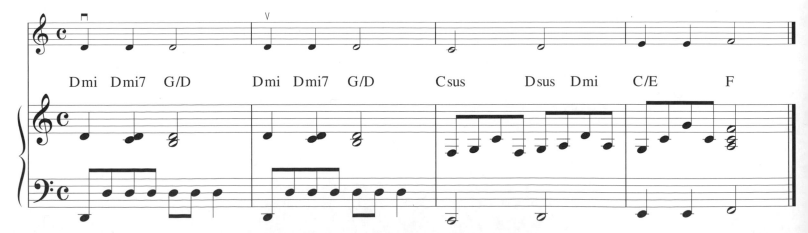

148. SIDE BY SIDE

149. C MAJOR SCALE

150. RHYTHM RAP

151. SLOW BOWS

152. LONG LONG AGO

T. H. Baily

Moderato

153. C MAJOR SCALE AND ARPEGGIO

154. LISTEN TO OUR SECTIONS

155. MONDAY'S MELODY

156. LET'S READ "E"

157. LET'S READ "A"

158. LET'S READ "G"

159. LET'S READ "F#" (F-sharp)

160. MOVING ALONG

161. G MAJOR SCALE

162. SHEPHERD'S HEY

English Folk Song

163. BIG ROCK CANDY MOUNTAIN

American Folk Song

164. LET'S READ "B"

165. ICE SKATING

Moderato

166. ESSENTIAL ELEMENTS QUIZ – ACADEMIC FESTIVAL OVERTURE THEME

Johannes Brahms

Moderato

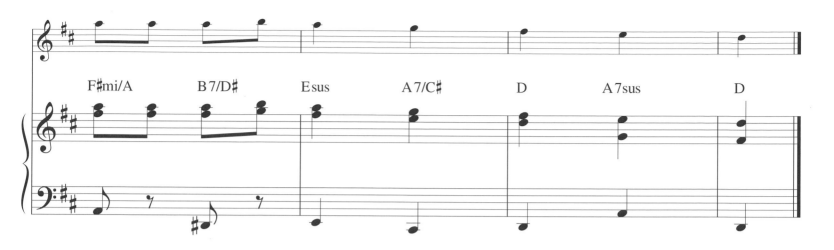

167. PLAY STACCATO

168. ARKANSAS TRAVELER

Allegro

Southern American Folk Song

169.

170.

174. HOOKED ON D MAJOR

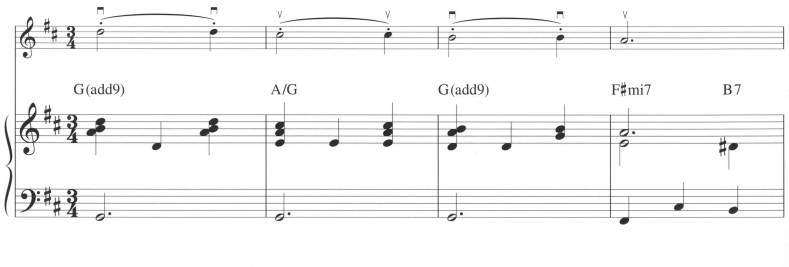

175. WALTZING BOWS

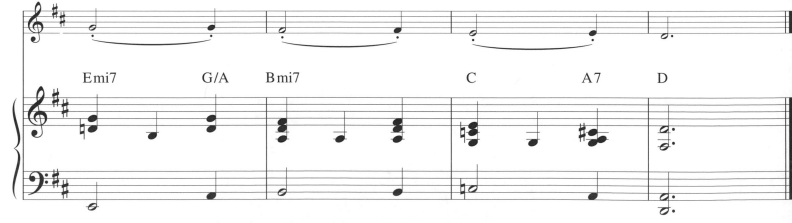

176. POP GOES THE WEASEL

American Folk Song

181. FORTE AND PIANO

Student books have repeats, not 1st and 2nd endings.

182. SURPRISE SYMPHONY THEME

Franz Josef Haydn

183. D MAJOR

Student books have repeats, not 1st and 2nd endings.

184. G MAJOR

Student books have repeats, not 1st and 2nd endings.

185. G MAJOR

Student books have repeats, not 1st and 2nd endings.

186. C MAJOR

Student books have repeats, not 1st and 2nd endings.

187. C MAJOR

188. CRIPPLE CREEK – Orchestra Arrangement   (**A** = Melody and **B** = Harmony)

American Folk Song
Arr. Michael Allen

189. TEKELE LOMERIA – Orchestra Arrangement

Kenyan Warrior Song
Arr. John Higgins

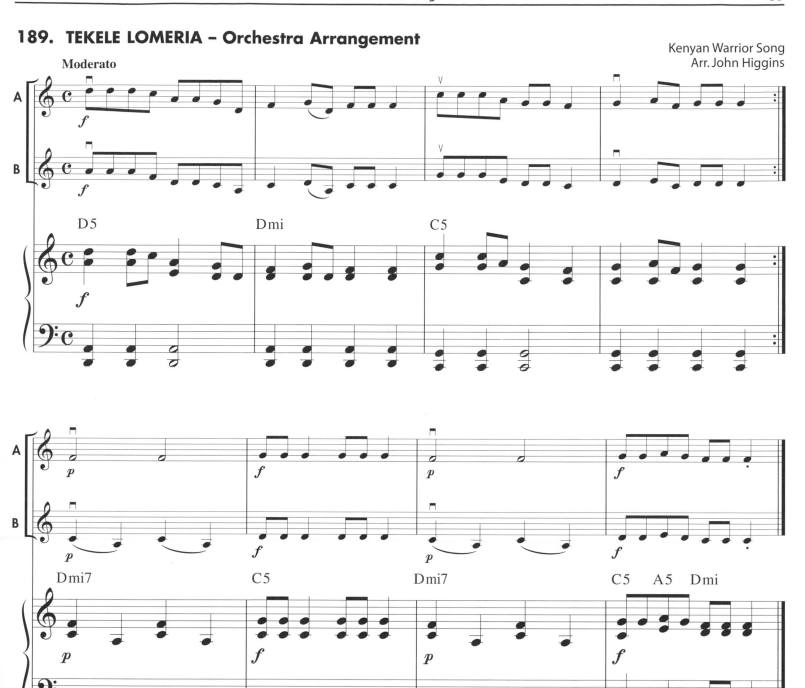

190. WILLIAM TELL OVERTURE – Orchestra Arrangement

Gioachino Rossini
Arr. John Higgins

191. ROCKIN' STRINGS – Orchestra Arrangement

John Higgins

192. SIMPLE GIFTS – Orchestra Arrangement

Shaker Folk Song
Arr. John Higgins

193. MINUET NO. 1 – Violin Solo

Johann Sebastian Bach
Arr. John Higgins

193. MINUET IN C – Viola Solo

Johann Sebastian Bach
Arr. John Higgins

193. MINUET NO. 2 – Cello Solo

Johann Sebastian Bach
Arr. John Higgins

193. MARCH IN D – Double Bass Solo

Johann Sebastian Bach
Arr. John Higgins

194. RHYTHM JAM – *Student books have an improvisation exercise.*

195. INSTANT MELODY – *Student books have an improvisation exercise.*